DINOSAURS!

BRACHIOSAURUS
AND OTHER
LONG-NECKED HERBIVORES

by
David West

Gareth Stevens
Publishing

Please visit our Web site, www.garethstevens.com.
For a free color catalog of all our high-quality books,
call toll free 1-800-542-2595 or fax 1-877-542-2596.

Library of Congress Cataloging-in-Publication Data

West, David, 1956-
Brachiosaurus and other long-necked herbivores / David West.
p. cm. — (Dinosaurs!)
Includes index.
ISBN 978-1-4339-4222-8 (pbk.)
ISBN 978-1-4339-4223-5 (6-pack)
ISBN 978-1-4339-4221-1 (lib. bdg.)
1. Brachiosaurus—Juvenile literature. 2. Herbivores, Fossil—Juvenile literature. I. Title.
QE862.S3W465 2011
567.913—dc22
2010009748

First Edition

Published in 2011 by
Gareth Stevens Publishing
111 East 14th Street, Suite 349
New York, NY 10003

Copyright © 2011 David West Books

Designed by David West Books
Editor: Ronne Randall

Printed in China

0456

CPSIA compliance information: Batch #DS10GS: For further information contact Gareth Stevens, New York, New York at 1-800-542-2595.

Contents

TAIL SPIKES
Some early sauropods had tail spikes or clubs at the end of their tails.

*This is Shunosaurus, a sauropod from Middle Jurassic China. Many **fossil** skeletons have been found, making it one of the best-studied sauropods.*

LONG TAIL
One of the main features of a sauropod was its long tail. Some had tails so long they could be used like whips. **Paleontologists** think that they could stand on their back legs, placing their tail on the ground to balance, so they could reach branches higher up.

What Is a Long-Necked **Herbivore**?

The dinosaurs in this book all belong to the **sauropod** group—plant-eating dinosaurs that had long tails and necks, and walked on four legs. They are notable for the enormous sizes that some species grew to, making them the largest animals ever to have lived on land. They resembled the closely related group **prosauropods**, which are also included in this book.

CLAWS
Claws on the back legs may have been used for defense against an attacker.

*Dinosaurs lived throughout the Mesozoic Era, which is divided into three periods, shown here. It is sometimes called the Age of the Reptiles. Dinosaurs first appeared in the Upper Triassic period and died out during a **mass extinction event** 65 million years ago.*

SPINES
Many sauropods had spines sticking out of their backs. Some even had two sets of spines.

HEAD
The heads of these dinosaurs were very small compared with the rest of the body.

BRAIN
These dinosaurs had very small brains. Some had to have large nerve groupings near their hips to help control movement.

TEETH
Their teeth were often peglike, so they could strip leaves from branches. They swallowed their food whole because they could not chew.

LONG NECK
Their long necks allowed them to browse on plants higher up and so avoid competing with other, smaller plant eaters.

FORELIMBS
Many sauropods had a single claw on each front foot. They might have used them to grip trees while feeding or as a form of defense.

DIGESTION
Polished stones found with some fossils suggest that sauropods swallowed stones to help mash up their food in their stomach. Some paleontologists disagree and suggest that the stones were swallowed accidentally.

SIZE
These monsters could reach lengths of 130 feet (40 m), as in the case of *Supersaurus,* and weigh up to 90–110 tons (82–100 metric tons), as with *Argentinosaurus*. A cow is shown as a visual scale guide.

227	205	180	159	144	98	65 Millions of years ago (mya)
Upper	Lower	Middle	Upper	Lower	Upper	
TRIASSIC		JURASSIC		CRETACEOUS		

Lower Cretaceous
132–127 mya
Argentina

Amargasaurus

Amargasaurus is named after a valley in Argentina where its fossils were discovered. It was a small to medium-sized sauropod with a long, whiplike tail similar to that of *Diplodocus* and a relatively short neck.

This was one of the strangest-looking sauropods ever discovered. Unlike all other sauropods, *Amargasaurus* had long spine bones sticking upward out of its neck and hip. Scientists think they may have been covered by flesh to create an enlarged, thin area that made the

A group of amargasaurs roam over the lip of a volcanic crater in this scene from Lower Cretaceous South America. Three Thalassodromeuses, *large* **pterosaurs**, *glide on thermals in the sky above.*

neck and back look big. Appearing bigger than it was could have been the dinosaur's form of defense. Only the largest **predators** would have attempted to attack an *Amargasaurus*. This enlarged area may also have helped **regulate** body temperature, like a radiator, or was perhaps used in mating rituals. The skin might have changed color in order to **communicate**, like a **chameleon's**.

Amargasaurus grew up to 39 feet (12 m) long and weighed around 5.5 tons (5 metric tons).

Anchisaurus

Anchisaurus, meaning "near lizard," was one of the first dinosaurs to be discovered. It was a small dinosaur for a sauropod. It spent most of its time on four feet but could rear up on its hind legs to reach higher plants.

Scientists think *Anchisaurus* was a transition between two-legged plant eaters and large four-legged sauropods. As a two-legged/four-legged crossover, *Anchisaurus* had to have multipurpose front feet. As hands, they could be used for grasping. They had a simple **reversible** first

A group of anchisaurs gather around a water hole in Lower Jurassic America. One of them chases a dragonfly. Paleontologists think that Anchisaurus *may have been an* **omnivore** *(eating meat, such as insects, as well as plants).*

finger, similar to a thumb, which had a large, curved claw. This could have been used in self-defense. As feet, the five toes could be placed flat against the ground, and they had strong ankles. *Anchisaurus* would have been quick on its feet, because it was **prey** to meat eaters like *Megapnosaurus* and *Dilophosaurus*. The teeth were blunt but had file-like edges, suggesting that mostly plants were eaten.

Anchisaurus was about 6.6 feet (2 m) long and would have weighed around 60 pounds (27 kg).

Brachiosaurus

Brachiosaurus means "arm lizard." It was given its name because its front "arm" limbs were longer than its back limbs. It is one of the largest animals to have walked the earth and has become one of the most recognized of all dinosaurs worldwide.

Unlike other sauropods, it had a giraffelike build, with long forelimbs and a very long neck. *Brachiosaurus* had teeth that resembled **chisels**, which were well suited to its herbivorous diet. The daily energy

An Archaeopteryx *catches the eye of a* Brachiosaurus *as a herd makes it way through a forest of conifers, grazing on the needle-shaped leaves, in this scene from Upper Jurassic Europe. One of them rears up on its hind legs to reach branches higher up.*

demands of *Brachiosaurus* would have been huge. It would have needed to eat more than 400 pounds (182 kg) of food per day. *Brachiosaurus* probably moved in herds, although fully grown individuals had little to fear from even the largest predators of the time, *Allosaurus* and *Torvosaurus*, because of their giant size.

Brachiosaurus grew up to 82 feet (25 m) long and weighed around 77 tons (70 metric tons).

Middle Jurassic
170–160 mya
England

Cetiosaurus

Cetiosaurus, meaning "whale lizard," was so named because its discoverer thought it was a sea creature. Its neck and tail were shorter than those of many other sauropods. It was the first sauropod to be discovered, 32 years before anyone had heard of dinosaurs.

The most unusual feature of this medium-sized sauropod is its backbone. Unlike most other sauropods, which had hollow vertebrae (which helped reduce their weight), this large herbivore had vertebrae

*In a scene from Middle Jurassic Europe, a Cetiosaurus covers her nest of eggs with ferns. A group of **inquisitive** coelurosaurs investigate, but at only 3 feet (1 m) long, they present little danger.*

of solid bone. Some paleontologists think that these giant dinosaurs roamed the plains of Jurassic Europe in large herds, moving at the brisk pace of 10 mph (16 km/h). Sauropods like *Cetiosaurus* laid a large clutch of soccer-ball-sized eggs. It is unlikely that they stayed around to look after them. The egg's structure was very strong, making it difficult to break into but easy to hatch out of.

Cetiosaurus could grow up to 59 feet (18 m) long and weighed around 27.3 tons (24.8 metric tons).

Upper Jurassic
150–135 mya
Tanzania

Dicraeosaurus

Dicraeosaurus was a small diplodocid that had many physical differences from the rest of the family. Its name means "double-headed lizard." It was named for the double row of spines along its back. These spines were shaped like a letter Y.

Unlike most diplodocids, *Dicraeosaurus* had a large head with a short, wide neck. Its tail was also short for a diplodocid, but it still might have been used as a whip (see pp. 16–17) to discourage predators.

14

*A **juvenile** Kentrosaurus feeds on the lower-lying plants among a group of **browsing** Dicraeosauruses in this scene from Upper Jurassic Africa. Rhamphorhynchuses flutter around their heads to catch flying insects disturbed by the feeding dinosaurs.*

Carnivores such as *Ceratosaurus* and *Elaphrosaurus* may have attacked small sauropods such as *Dicraeosaurus,* especially if they hunted in packs. *Dicraeosaurus* lived alongside the plated dinosaur *Kentrosaurus* and the giant sauropod *Giraffatitan*. These dinosaurs were able to live together without competing for food because the difference in their sizes meant they could feed at different levels. *Dicraeosaurus* would have grazed on the middle layer of plants.

Dicraeosaurus grew up to 41 feet (12 m) long and weighed up to 6 tons (5.4 metric tons).

15

Diplodocus

Diplodocus, meaning "double beam," had **double-beamed** bones located along the underside of the tail. It is one of the longest dinosaurs ever found. Its neck contained 15 bones, and the tail had up to 90, although a complete tail has never been found.

Diplodocus may have used its long tail like a whip to scare away predators. Paleontologists think it may also have been used for communication in the way cats and dogs use their tails today.

A *herd* of Diplodocuses *trundle across the floor of a dried-up lake in search of food in this scene from Upper Jurassic North America.* Diplodocus *may have traveled in herds,* **migrating** *when the local food supply was depleted.*

Diplodocus had a very long neck, possibly used to poke into forests to get foliage. Alternatively, the long neck may have enabled this sauropod to eat soft horsetails, club mosses, and ferns that grew in boggy areas, where a heavy sauropod would get stuck. But *Diplodocus* could stand on firm ground and stretch its long neck to browse these areas safely.

Diplodocus was about 89 feet (27 m) long and weighed around 24 tons (21.8 metric tons).

Europasaurus

Europasaurus, "Europe lizard," was very different from other sauropods. Although related to the giant sauropod *Brachiosaurus*, *Europasaurus* was actually very small. Paleontologists think it was once large but **evolved** into a form of dwarf sauropod.

On small islands, where there were fewer sources of food, evolution would force large animal life to shrink. This probably happened to *Europasaurus*, the smallest sauropod. It is likely that it lived on a small

An adult Europasaurus *looks down on a juvenile while an* Archaeopteryx *glides in the foreground. This scene is set on the coast of an island within the Lower Saxony basin in Upper Jurassic Europe.*

chain of islands, the largest of these having an area of only 124,300 square miles (200,000 sq km). This would not have been big enough to support large sauropods for long. Fossils of a herd of *Europasaurus* were discovered in a **bone bed**. One suggestion has been that the herd was swept out to sea from a beach, perhaps by a **tsunami**. They would have drowned before becoming buried in the seabed.

Europasaurus was about 19 feet (5.7 m) long and weighed around 3 tons (2.7 metric tons).

Lower Jurassic
208–204 mya
Lesotho, South Africa, Zimbabwe

Massospondylus

Massospondylus, "longer backbone," was one of the first dinosaurs to be named. It was a medium-sized prosauropod, and it walked on two legs. Paleontologists think it was probably a plant eater, although some suggest it might have been an omnivore.

Massospondylus, like most prosauropods, had a slender body and long neck. Each of its forefeet had a sharp thumb claw that was used in defense or possibly feeding. Recent studies show that *Massospondylus*

A group of Massospondyluses ***graze*** *on plants in this scene from Lower Jurassic Africa. One* Massospondylus *looks around at a young* Syntarsus *chasing a group of* Lesothosauruses *in the foreground.*

grew steadily throughout its life span. It had air sacs similar to those of birds, which helped it breathe in the low-oxygen atmosphere. Studies also show that it may have cared for its young. With slender, powerful back legs, it was a swift runner. Speed would have been necessary to evade predators such as *Syntarsus*, a lightly built **theropod**.

Massospondylus was about 13 feet (4 m) long and weighed around 1.5 tons (1.4 metric tons).

21

Omeisaurus

Omeisaurus was named after the sacred mountain Omeishan in China, where it was discovered. It had an extremely long neck, with several more neck bones (17) than average sauropods. The neck was over half the length of the entire dinosaur.

Omeisaurus had a deep, blunt head and spoon-shaped teeth for eating plants. Its size probably protected it from attack by predatory dinosaurs, but *Omeisaurus* may have had something else to protect it.

22

A group of three Omeisauruses use their incredibly long necks to graze among the highest branches of a mixed fern and conifer forest in this scene from Middle Jurassic Asia.

Paleontologists working on the sauropod *Shunosaurus* (see pp. 24–25) discovered that its tail ended in a large, bony club, like that of the **ankylosaurids**. They found more tail clubs, of a different shape, in the same locations as *Omeisaurus*. Some Chinese paleontologists think they may belong to *Omeisaurus*. But an *Omeisaurus* skeleton with the tail club attached must be found for scientists to be sure.

Omeisaurus was about 66 feet (20 m) long and weighed around 4 tons (3.6 metric tons).

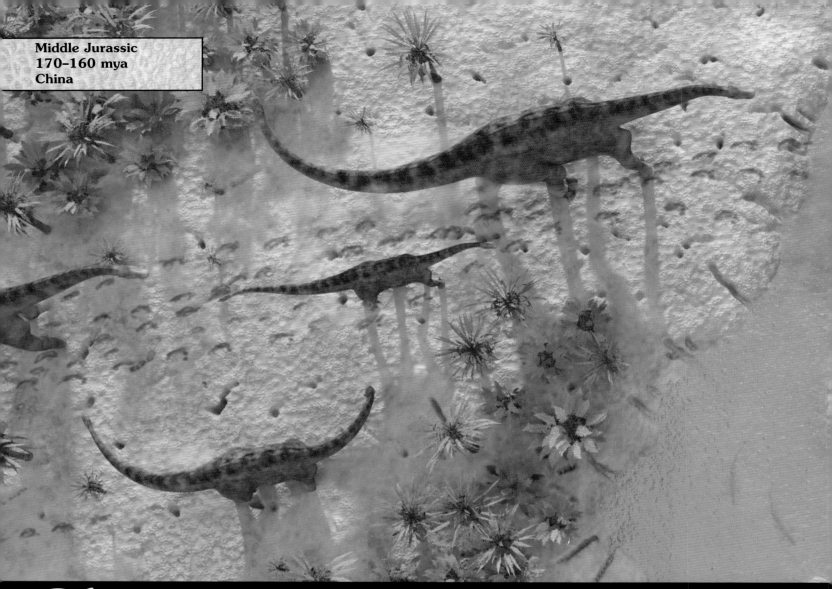

Shunosaurus

Shunosaurus was named after Sichuan Province in China, where its fossils were found. It is known from more than twenty near-complete skeletons, making it **anatomically** one of the best-known sauropods.

Shunosaurus shared the Asian Middle Jurassic landscape with other sauropods such as *Datousaurus*, *Omeisaurus*, *Protognathosaurus*, and the early **stegosaur** *Huayangosaurus*. *Shunosaurus* may have roamed in large herds. With its long, thick neck, it could feed on plants

24

A group of Shunosauruses *travel across a landscape crisscrossed with river channels in this scene from Middle Jurassic Asia. Many fossil skeletons have been found together, suggesting that these dinosaurs lived in large herds.*

and leaves high above the ground that most other herbivores could not reach. Its large body, weighing about a ton, made it safe from attack by most predators, such as *Gasosaurus*. If it was attacked, it could defend itself with its tail, which ended in a large, bony club with two pairs of short spikes. *Shunosaurus* is unusual, as tail clubs are rarely found on sauropods.

Shunosaurus was about 40 feet (12 m) long and weighed about 1 ton (0.9 metric ton).

25

Spinophorosaurus

Spinophorosaurus, "spine-bearing lizard," is a very recent discovery of a new kind of sauropod that lived in what is now Africa. Its fossils may reveal a connection between North African, European, and east Asian sauropods during the Jurassic period.

Spinophorosaurus is the most complete early sauropod found so far. Although not the largest long-necked dinosaur *ever* to have lived, it still would have made a cow look like a child's toy.

A Spinophorosaurus uses its tail spikes to defend itself from a hungry Megalosaurus-like theropod in this scene from Middle Jurassic Africa. Fossils of Spinophorosaurus were discovered in 2009 in Niger, Africa.

This new sauropod was unusual in that it had a set of spikes at the end of its tail called "thagomizers," just like *Stegosaurus*. These two pairs of large, bony spikes were used as defense against predators. This form of defensive weaponry is also found on *Shunosaurus*, a sauropod with a spiked tail club that lived around the same time in what is now China (see pp. 24–25).

Spinophorosaurus grew to 43 feet (13 m) in length and weighed 9 tons (8.2 metric tons).

Titanosaurus

Titanosaurus, meaning "titan lizard," was named after the ancient Greek **mythological** race of giants called Titans. These huge plant eaters could be found around the globe and continued to live right up to the mass extinction event 65 million years ago.

Titanosaurus was from the same family as *Argentinosaurus.* It was probably related to dinosaurs that traveled from South America when it was still connected to Africa. The entire family of these Cretaceous

Three Titanosauruses cross a shallow sea to reach new feeding grounds in this scene from Upper Cretaceous Asia. Their fossils are scattered and incomplete, with no intact skulls, so reconstructing what these beasts looked like has taken a lot of guesswork.

giants is named after *Titanosaurus*. It was a heavily built sauropod, and it is believed that most had tough, bony plates covering their bodies. There is evidence that some titanosaurs may have roamed in herds of dozens or hundreds of adults and juveniles. The discovery of nesting grounds (complete with fossilized eggs) suggests that females may have laid their eggs in groups for protection.

Titanosaurus grew up to 65 feet (19.8 m) long and weighed around 15 tons (13.6 metric tons).

Animal Gallery

Other dinosaurs and animals that appear in the scenes.

Coelosaur
(pp. 12–13)
Theropod (two-legged
carnivorous dinosaur)
Middle Jurassic
Europe

Rhamphorhynchus
(pp. 14–15)
"beak snout"
Pterosaur (flying reptile)
Upper Jurassic
Germany, Portugal,
Spain, Tanzania, UK

Archaeopteryx
(pp. 10, 11, 18, 19)
"ancient wing"
Early bird
Upper Jurassic
Germany

Lesothosaurus (pp. 20–21)
"lizard from Lesotho"
(beaked, herbivorous dinosaur)
Lower Jurassic
Lesotho

Thalassodromeus (pp. 6–7)
"sea runner"
Pterosaur (flying reptile)
Lower Cretaceous
Brazil

Syntarsus (pp. 20–21)
"fused ankle"
Theropod (two-legged
carnivorous dinosaur)
Upper Triassic
South Africa, USA,
Zimbabwe

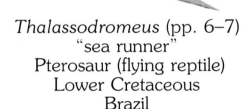

Kentrosaurus (pp. 14–15)
"spiked lizard"
Stegosaurid (herbivorous dinosaur
with plates and spikes)
Upper Jurassic
Tanzania

Megalosaurus (pp. 26–27)
"big lizard"
Theropod (two-legged
carnivorous dinosaur)
Middle Jurassic
England, France, Portugal

Glossary

anatomically Relating to all parts of an animal's body.

ankylosaurid A member of a group of plant-eating dinosaurs with a low, thick body and a bony club at the end of the tail.

bone bed A layer of rock that contains bones or fossilized bones.

browsing Moving around while eating.

carnivore A meat-eating animal.

chameleon A modern lizard that can change color.

chisel A tool for chipping and shaping wood, which is sharpened at the end of its long, bevel-edged blade.

communicate To send or express an emotion or feeling.

double-beamed Two pairs of beamlike bones.

evolved To have changed by natural selection over a long period of time.

fossil The remains of a living thing that have turned to rock.

graze To feed on growing plants.

herbivore A plant eater.

inquisitive Curious.

juvenile A youngster.

mass extinction event A widespread disappearance of species of animals and plants in a relatively short period of time.

migrating Moving from one place to another, either for a short seasonal period, or forever.

mythological Relating to stories and legends from the past.

omnivore An animal that eats both plants and meat.

paleontologist A scientist who studies life forms that existed in earlier geologic periods by looking at fossils.

predator An animal that hunts and kills other animals for food.

prey An animal that is hunted by carnivores.

prosauropod A member of a group of a dinosaurs that were originally thought to be the ancestors of the sauropods, but are now considered a parallel lineage. They had a long neck, forelimbs shorter than hind limbs, and a very large thumb claw for defense.

pterosaur A member of the flying reptiles that lived during the age of the dinosaurs.

regulate Adjust to a certain amount.

reversible Able to change back.

sauropod A member of a group of large, four-legged, plant-eating dinosaurs that had very long necks.

stegosaur A member of a family of plated dinosaurs that includes *Stegosaurus*.

theropod A member of a two-legged dinosaur family that includes most of the giant carnivorous dinosaurs.

tsunami A giant wave that crashes onto coastal and low-lying land, usually caused by an earthquake under the seabed.

Index